MEDITATIONS ON
THE PSALMS

Psalms 38-75 taken from the New International Version
Comment by E M Blaiklock Photographs by Gordon Gray

SCRIPTURE UNION

Published by
SCRIPTURE UNION
47 Marylebone Lane London W1M 6AX

Text of the Psalms from
the New International Version of the Bible © UK 1979
by the New York International Bible Society
and used by permission
Commentary © Scripture Union Books Ltd 1979
Photographs © Scripture Union Books Ltd 1979

ISBN 0 85421 832 7

Books in this series
Book 1 Psalms   1-37
Book 2 Psalms   38-75
Book 3 Psalms   76-111
Book 4 Psalms 112-150

Designed by Tony Cantale

Printed in England by W.S. Cowell Ltd,
Buttermarket, Ipswich.

Book 1 ISBN 0 85421 798 3

Book 2 ISBN 0 85421 832 7

Book 3 ISBN 0 85421 833 5

Book 4 ISBN 0 85421 834 3

38 DISCIPLINE

¹O LORD, do not rebuke me in your anger
  or discipline me in your wrath.
²For your arrows have pierced me,
  and your hand has come down upon me.
³Because of your wrath there is no health in my body;
  my bones have no soundness because of my sin.
⁴My guilt has overwhelmed me
  like a burden too heavy to bear.

⁵My wounds fester and are loathsome
  because of my sinful folly.
⁶I am bowed down and brought very low;
  all day long I go about mourning.
⁷My back is filled with searing pain;
  there is no health in my body.
⁸I am feeble and utterly crushed;
  I groan in anguish of heart.

⁹All my longings lie open before you, O Lord;
  my sighing is not hidden from you.
¹⁰My heart pounds, my strength fails me;
  even the light has gone from my eyes.
¹¹My friends and companions avoid me
  because of my wounds;
  my neighbours stay far away.
¹²Those who seek my life set their traps,
  those who would harm me talk of my ruin;
  all day long they plot deception.

¹³I am like a deaf man, who cannot hear,
  like a mute, who cannot open his mouth;
¹⁴I have become like a man who does not hear,
  whose mouth can offer no reply.
¹⁵I wait for you, O LORD;
  you will answer, O LORD, my God.
¹⁶For I said, 'Do not let them gloat
  or exalt themselves over me when my foot slips.'

¹⁷For I am about to fall,
  and my pain is ever with me.
¹⁸I confess my iniquity;
  I am troubled by my sin.
¹⁹Many are those who are my vigorous enemies;
  those who hate me without reason are numerous.
²⁰Those who repay my good with evil
  slander me when I seek what is good.

²¹O LORD, do not forsake me;
  be not far from me, O my God.
²²Come quickly to help me,
  O Lord my Saviour.

Physical and mental agony, fruit of sin and folly (3, 5), have shocked, burdened, pained (1, 2, 4, 6). Job only holds such words of sorrow, and Job was not deserted (11), nor ravaged by foes, as David was (12). Wounded, he reaches for the healer (9, 15). Indeed, hideously exposed to malice, he cries desperately for help (9, 15-22).

Perhaps this, third of the 'penitential' psalms goes with the fourth (Psalm 51). There is one escape—God.

39 IN SILENCE

¹I said, 'I will watch my ways
and keep my tongue from sin;
I will put a muzzle on my mouth
as long as the wicked are in my
presence.'
²But when I was silent and still,
not even saying anything good,
my anguish increased.
³My heart grew hot within me,
and as I meditated, the fire burned;
then I spoke with my tongue:

⁴'Show me, O LORD, my life's end
and the number of my days;
let me know how fleeting is my life.
⁵You have made my days a mere
handbreadth;
the span of my years is as nothing before
you.
Each man's life is but a breath.   *Selah*
⁶Man is a mere phantom as he goes to and
fro:
He bustles about, but only in vain;
he heaps up wealth, not knowing who
will get it.

⁷'But now, Lord, what do I look for?
My hope is in you.

⁸Save me from all my transgressions;
do not make me the scorn of fools.
⁹I was silent; I would not open my mouth,
for you are the one who has done this.
¹⁰Remove your scourge from me;
I am overcome by the blow of your hand.
¹¹You rebuke and discipline men for their
sin;
you consume their wealth like a moth—
each man is but a breath.   *Selah*

¹²'Hear my prayer, O LORD,
listen to my cry for help;
be not deaf to my weeping.
For I dwell with you as an alien,
a stranger, as all my fathers were.
¹³Look away from me, that I may rejoice
again
before I depart and am no more.'

*Verbal echoes of Psalm 38 mark this
psalm as a companion piece, a quieter
expression of the same desperate
experience of sin and penitence. Some
measure of peace has come. The sufferer
has tried to hide his agony from others
(1), lest the ill-wisher triumph. He was
even silent before the good who might
have helped (2), until he saw, with acute
insight, that such suppression burned the
mind.*

*He found relief in prayer, quieter now
and more reflective, remembering the
brevity of life, and the vanity of earthly
things (4-6). Life was worthless unless
God made it radiant (7) and quenched the
scorn of fools (8). And yet, how richly had
he deserved chastisement (9-11). The
ending is deep in pathos. How gratefully
should the Christian grasp the hope that
came with a risen Christ. To the Old
Testament it was no more than fleeting
vision.*

40 FROM THE PIT

I waited patiently for the LORD;
   he turned to me and heard my cry.
²He lifted me out of the slimy pit,
   out of the mud and mire;
he set my feet on a rock
   and gave me a firm place to stand.
³He put a new song in my mouth,
   a hymn of praise to our God.

Many will see and fear
   and put their trust in the LORD.

⁴Blessed is the man
   who makes the LORD his trust,
who does not look to the proud,
   to those who turn aside to false gods.
⁵Many, O LORD my God,
   are the wonders you have done.
The things you planned for us

no one can recount to you;
were I to speak and tell of them,
   they would be too many to declare.

[6] Sacrifice and offering you did not desire,
   but my ears you have pierced;
burnt offerings and sin offerings
   you did not require.
[7] Then I said, 'Here I am, I have come—
   it is written about me in the scroll.
[8] To do your will, O my God, is my desire;
   your law is within my heart.'

[9] I proclaim righteousness in the great
     assembly;
   I do not seal my lips,
   as you know, O LORD.
[10] I do not hide your righteousness in my
     heart;
   I speak of your faithfulness and
     salvation.
I do not conceal your love and your truth
   from the great assembly.

[11] Do not withhold your mercy from me, O
     LORD;
   may your love and your truth always
     protect me.
[12] For troubles without number surround
     me;
   my sins have overtaken me, and I cannot
     see.
They are more than the hairs of my head,
   and my heart fails within me.

[13] Be pleased, O LORD, to save me;
   O LORD, come quickly to help me.
[14] May all who seek to take my life
   be put to shame and confusion;
may all who desire my ruin be turned
     back in disgrace.
[15] May those who say to me, 'Aha! Aha!'
   be appalled at their own shame.
[16] But may all who seek you
   rejoice and be glad in you;
may those who love your salvation always
     say
   'The LORD be exalted!'

[17] Yet I am poor and needy;
   may the Lord think of me.
You are my help and my deliverer;
   O my God, do not delay.

*The five psalms, 37-41, form a sequence
and were deliberately arranged. It might
be guessed that they all follow in the
months which began sombrely with Psalm
51. They form a prayer book for any
defeated Christian groping desperately
back to God.*

*God has 'bent down' and answered (1).
It was like being lifted out of some slimy
pit, with something new and beautiful to
say (Psalm 51.13). The 'new song' is the
next eight verses. But the consequences
of royal sin are yet to be faced, for when
God forgives and forgets, often men do
not (12-15). He, the king, can see his
poverty and need, he is a fragile thing as
his fall has so abundantly revealed. Here
is humility, the first pathway to the
restoration of godliness. The trial is not
ended. There is still the test of God's
seeming delay. But the battle is won.*

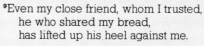

41 CARE FOR THE WEAK

Blessed is he who has regard for the weak;
the LORD delivers him in times of trouble.
²The LORD will protect him and preserve his life;
he will bless him in the land
and not surrender him to the desire of his foes.
³The LORD will sustain him on his sickbed
and restore him from his bed of illness.

⁴I said, 'O LORD, have mercy on me;
heal me, for I have sinned against you.'
⁵My enemies say of me in malice,
'When will he die and his name perish?'
⁶Whenever one comes to see me,
he speaks falsely, while his heart gathers slander;
then he goes out and spreads it abroad.

⁷All my enemies whisper together against me;
they imagine the worst for me, saying,
⁸'A vile disease has beset him;
he will never get up from the place where he lies.'

⁹Even my close friend, whom I trusted,
he who shared my bread,
has lifted up his heel against me.

¹⁰But you, O LORD, have mercy on me;
raise me up, that I may repay them.
¹¹I know that you are pleased with me,
for my enemy does not triumph over me.
¹²In my integrity you uphold me
and set me in your presence for ever.

¹³Praise be to the LORD, the God of Israel,
from everlasting to everlasting.
Amen and Amen.

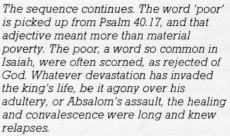

The sequence continues. The word 'poor' is picked up from Psalm 40.17, and that adjective meant more than material poverty. The poor, a word so common in Isaiah, were often scorned, as rejected of God. Whatever devastation has invaded the king's life, be it agony over his adultery, or Absalom's assault, the healing and convalescence were long and knew relapses.

The psalm closes with a benediction, probably from the hand of the compiler. In it he reveals how the book has moved him. Especially he has lived with a great human being, a man of heights and depths, of deep and wonderful insights and dark despairs, a man like any one of us, exalted by persecution or crushed by it, but a man above all who laid all his joys and sorrows at the feet of God. We can do no other, if we would have them sanctified and turn to usefulness.

9

42 THIRSTY FOR GOD

As the deer pants for streams of
    water,
  so my soul pants for you, O God.
²My soul thirsts for God, for the living God.
  When can I go and meet with God?
³My tears have been my food day and
    night,
  while men say to me all day long,
    'Where is your God?'
⁴These things I remember
    as I pour out my soul:
  how I used to go with the multitude,
    leading the procession to the house of
      God,
  with shouts of joy and thanksgiving
    among the festive throng.

⁵Why are you downcast, O my soul?
    Why so disturbed within me?
  Put your hope in God,
    for I will yet praise him,
    my Saviour and my God.

⁶My soul is downcast within me;
    therefore I will remember you
  from the land of the Jordan,
    the heights of Hermon—from Mount
      Mizar.
⁷Deep calls to deep
    in the roar of your waterfalls;
  all your waves and breakers
    have swept over me.

⁸By day the LORD directs his love,
    at night his song is with me—
  a prayer to the God of my life.

⁹I say to God my Rock,
    'Why have you forgotten me?
  Why must I go about mourning,
    oppressed by the enemy?'
¹⁰My bones suffer mortal agony
    as my foes taunt me,
  saying to me all day long,
    'Where is your God?'

¹¹Why are you downcast, O my soul?
    Why so disturbed within me?
  Put your hope in God,
    for I will yet praise him,
    my Saviour and my God.

*This psalm, which once was made one
psalm along with the next, could be the
bitter lamentation of poor Jehoiachin
(2 Kings 24.11-15), who was carried off to
exile in Babylon, or of some other captive
or refugee from tyranny. The scene seems
to have been in the north-west (6), in the
region of the Damascus road.*

*It is bitter in such days of agony to
remember happier things (4), the old
ways of peace before the storms of war, to
look down from the arid, weary road on a
stormy wind churning Galilee, and see in
its watery tumult the tumult of the soul (7).*

*God seemed far off as the blessed
temple, a charred ruin, was left further
and further behind (1, 2). The guards
sneer at the helpless Jews (10), and like a
refrain, the captive repeats an agonised
question: Why, why, why? (5, 11). He must
hope, he tells himself, or die of thirst for
God (1, 2). Surely, surely it will end . . .*

43 PRAYER FOR LIGHT

Vindicate me, O God,
and plead my cause against an ungodly
nation;
rescue me from deceitful and wicked
men.
²You are God my stronghold.
Why have you rejected me?
Why must I go about mourning,
oppressed by the enemy?
³Send forth your light and your truth,
let them guide me;
let them bring me to your holy mountain
to the place where you dwell.
⁴Then will I go to the altar of God,
to God, my joy and my delight.
I will praise you with the harp,
O God, my God.

⁵Why are you downcast, O my soul?
Why so disturbed within me?
Put your hope in God,
for I will yet praise him,
my Saviour and my God.

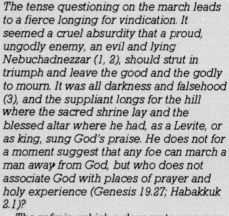

*The tense questioning on the march leads
to a fierce longing for vindication. It
seemed a cruel absurdity that a proud,
ungodly enemy, an evil and lying
Nebuchadnezzar (1, 2), should strut in
triumph and leave the good and the godly
to mourn. It was all darkness and falsehood
(3), and the supplicant longs for the hill
where the sacred shrine lay and the
blessed altar where he had, as a Levite, or
as king, sung God's praise. He does not for
a moment suggest that any foe can march a
man away from God, but who does not
associate God with places of prayer and
holy experience (Genesis 19.27; Habakkuk
2.1)?*

*The refrain, which a desperate man was
training himself to say, in tune with his
trudging feet: 'Hope, hope, hope . . . ' It is
all faith can grasp at. Some day, some day,
if God is, and surely he is, this horror will
pass away. In a bent and twisted landscape
of the soul where else but Godwards can a
man look?*

44 WE FACE DISASTER

We have heard with our ears, O God;
    our fathers have told us
what you did in their days,
    in days long ago.
²With your hand you drove out the nations
    and planted our fathers;
you crushed the peoples
    and made our fathers flourish.
³It was not by their swords that they won
        the land,
    nor did their arm bring them victory;
it was your right hand, your arm,
    and the light of your face,
    for you loved them.

⁴You are my King and my God,
    who decrees victories for Jacob.
⁵Through you we push back our enemies;
    through your name we trample our foes.
⁶I do not trust in my bow,
    my sword does not bring me victory;
⁷but you give us victory over our enemies,
    you put our adversaries to shame.
⁸In God we make our boast all day long,
    and we will praise your name for
        ever.   *Selah*

⁹But now you have rejected and humbled
        us;
    you no longer go out with our armies.
¹⁰You made us retreat before the enemy,
    and our adversaries have plundered us.
¹¹You gave us up to be devoured like
        sheep
    and have scattered us among the
        nations.
¹²You sold your people for a pittance,
    gaining nothing from their sale.

¹³You have made us a reproach to our
        neighbours,
    the scorn and derision of those around
        us.
¹⁴You have made us a byword among the
        nations;
    the people shake their heads at us.
¹⁵My disgrace is before me all day long,
    and my face is covered with shame
¹⁶at the taunts of those who reproach and
        revile me,
    because of the enemy, who is bent on
        revenge.

¹⁷All this happened to us,
    though we had not forgotten you
    or been false to your covenant.

¹⁸Our hearts had not turned back;
   our feet had not strayed from your path.
¹⁹But you crushed us and made us a haunt
      for jackals
   and covered us over with deep
      darkness.

²⁰If we had forgotten the name of our God
   or spread out our hands to a foreign god,
²¹would not God have discovered it,
   since he knows the secrets of the heart?
²²Yet for your sake we face death all day
      long;
   we are considered as sheep to be
      slaughtered.

²³Awake, O Lord! Why do you sleep?
   Rouse yourself! Do not reject us for ever.
²⁴Why do you hide your face
   and forget our misery and oppression?

²⁵We are brought down to the dust;
   our bodies cling to the ground.
²⁶Rise up and help us;
   redeem us because of your unfailing
      love.

*This hymn may have been a composition of
the 'sons of Korah', those custodians of the
temple music. It has been ascribed to times
as far apart as David's battles for secure
frontiers, to the times of the valiant
Maccabees, eight centuries later.*

*It was certainly a time of stress and it
might appear to belong rather to the days
of Isaiah or Jeremiah. It raises the old, old
question: 'Why does God allow the good to
suffer? Is all distress a punishment?' Let
God arise, as he is said to have done in
times past (1-8).*

*Had he changed? If so, why shame
before arrogant pagans? Calamity, in fact,
seemed to contradict the covenant
(Leviticus 26, Deuteronomy 28). It had come
in a time, it seemed, of faithfulness, not
apostasy. In forthright language (23-26) he
pleads and 'boldly approaches the eternal
throne'. There are testing times when a
man can only ride a wave of aggressive
doubt by faith and waiting (23-26).*

45 WEDDING SONG

My heart is stirred by a noble theme
as I recite my verses for the king;
my tongue is the pen of a skilful writer.

2 You are the most excellent of men
and your lips have been anointed with grace,
since God has blessed you for ever.
3 Gird your sword upon your side, O mighty one;
clothe yourself with splendour and majesty.
4 In your majesty ride forth victoriously
in behalf of truth, humility and righteousness;
let your right hand display awesome deeds.
5 Let your sharp arrows pierce the hearts of the king's enemies;
let the nations fall beneath your feet.
6 Your throne, O God, will last for ever and ever;
a sceptre of justice will be the sceptre of your kingdom.
7 You love righteousness and hate wickedness;
therefore God, your God, has set you above your companions
by anointing you with the oil of moy.
8 All your robes are fragrant with myrrh and aloes and cassia;
from palaces adorned with ivory
the music of the strings makes you glad.
9 Daughters of kings are among your honoured women;
at your right hand is the royal bride in gold of Ophir.

10 Listen, O daughter, consider and give ear:
forget your people and your father's house.
11 The king is enthralled by your beauty;
honour him, for he is your lord.
12 The Daughter of Tyre will come with a gift,
men of wealth will seek your favour.
13 All glorious is the princess within her chamber;
her gown is interwoven with gold.

14 In embroidered garments she is led to the king;
her virgin companions follow her and are brought to you.
15 They are led in with joy and gladness;
they enter the palace of the king.

16 Your sons will take the place of your fathers;
you will make them princes throughout the land.
17 I will perpetuate your memory through all generations;
therefore the nations will praise you for ever and ever.

This is a wedding song, to be set beside the Song of Solomon and the story of Cana as marks of God's approval on human love and marriage. A guess might be that it was written to order by one of the sons of Korah for the wedding of Jezebel's daughter Athaliah to Jehoram, son of Jehoshaphat. Ahab, father of Athaliah, had a palace with rooms lined with ivory (8). That the royal couple ,later provided some dark and evil pages of history, does not invalidate the guess. Marriage and royalty can begin in beauty and God's benediction, and end, like Eden, in evil and gloom.

Nor does the fact that verses 6 and 7 'burst their banks', and become in Hebrews 1.8,9, a reference to Christ, rule out the original intention.

Nor does poetry cease to be poetry, or a psalm lose claim to inspiration, if it is written deliberately to order. Inspiration demands only a surrendered mind, hands, skill. Why should a poet be less a tool of God than the builders of the tabernacle (Exodus 35.10-25, 30-35)?

46 WE WILL NOT FEAR

God is our refuge and strength,
an ever present help in trouble.
²Therefore we will not fear, though the
earth give way
and the mountains fall into the heart of
the sea,
³though its waters roar and foam
and the mountains quake with their
surging.   *Selah*

⁴There is a river whose streams make glad
the city of God,
the holy place where the Most High
dwells.
⁵God is within her, she will not fall;
God will help her at break of day.
⁶Nations are in uproar, kingdoms fall;
he lifts his voice, the earth melts.

⁷The LORD Almighty is with us;
the God of Jacob is our
fortress.   *Selah*

⁸Come and see the works of the LORD,
the desolations he has brought on the
earth.
⁹He makes wars cease to the ends of the
earth;
he breaks the bow and shatters the
spear,
he burns the shields with fire.
¹⁰'Be still, and know that I am God;
I will be exalted among the nations,
I will be exalted in the earth.'

¹¹The LORD Almighty is with us;
the God of Jacob is our
fortress.   *Selah*

Some peril has passed. Did Isaiah write this poem when the grim peril of Sennacherib died? (Isaiah 14.9-27; chapters 36, 37). Refuge in time of trouble is a universal longing (1), and lies are no refuge (Isaiah 28.15-17). When all that seems stable totters, God alone stands (2, 3).

Was verse 4 a reference to the engineering which brought Siloam's quiet stream (Isaiah 8.6) through a tunnel into Jerusalem? And was verse 6 a reference to the roaring army outside the walls, with verses 8 and 9 referring to how 'the angel of the Lord put to death a hundred and eighty-five thousand men'? (Isaiah 37.36). R.K. Harrison translates verse 10: 'Stop your striving, and recognise that I am God.' 'Give in,' says Moffatt boldly. There is sometimes nothing else to do.

47 SHOUTS OF JOY

Clap your hands, all you nations;
shout to God with cries of joy.
[2] How awesome is the LORD Most High,
the great King over all the earth!
[3] He subdued nations under us,
peoples under our feet.
[4] He chose our inheritance for us,
the pride of Jacob, whom he
loved.   *Selah*

[5] God has ascended amid shouts of joy,
the LORD amid the sounding of trumpets.
[6] Sing praises to God, sing praises;
sing praises to our King, sing praises.

[7] For God is the King of all the earth;
sing to him a psalm of praise.
[8] God reigns over the nations;
God is seated on his holy throne.
[9] The nobles of the nations assemble
as the people of the God of Abraham,
for the kings of the earth belong to God;
he is greatly exalted.

Here is the theme, whatever the historical background of Psalm 46 was, continued in jubilation. It was a hymn for some victory day from some devoted Korahite laureate. The vision of God as 'King of all the earth' (7) was one which haunted Isaiah, and Paul with his dream of the Empire for Christ. The last verse seems even to envisage Gentile adherents.

There is something beautiful taking shape in this burst of passionate and grateful devotion. Jubilation contains no note of arrogant triumph. Indeed there glistens through the glad words a vision of a world seeking God. As R.K. Harrison renders verse 9: 'The noble from pagan peoples assemble to be one with the people of the God of Abraham.' It is still the vision of the Church.

48 THE HOLY MOUNTAIN

Great is the LORD, and most worthy
   of praise,
in the city of our God, his holy mountain.
²It is beautiful in its loftiness,
   the joy of the whole earth.
Like the utmost heights of Zaphon is Mount
   Zion,
   the city of the great King.
³God is in her citadels;
   he has shown himself to be her fortress.

⁴When the kings joined forces,
   when they advanced together,
⁵they saw her and were astounded;
   they fled in terror.
⁶Trembling seized them there,
   pain like that of a woman in labour.
⁷You destroyed them like ships of Tarshish
   shattered by an east wind.

⁸As we have heard,
   so have we seen
in the city of the LORD Almighty,
   in the city of our God:
God makes her secure for
   ever.   *Selah*

⁹Within your temple, O God,
   we meditate on your unfailing love.
¹⁰Like your name, O God,
   your praise reaches to the ends of the
   earth;
   your right hand is filled with
   righteousness.
¹¹Mount Zion rejoices,
   the villages of Judah are glad
because of your judgments.

¹²Walk about Zion, go round her,
   count her towers,

¹³consider well her ramparts,
   view her citadels,
      that you may tell of them to the next
         generation.
¹⁴For this God is our God for ever and ever;
   he will be our guide even to the end.

The same subject continues, and looks very like the happy outcome of Sennacherib's invasion. The Assyrian king, whose story is told in his own words on the Taylor Prism, can hardly slur over the fact that he tried and failed to take Jerusalem.

   The city had her superb ridgetop situation to thank (1, 2). Verse 4 again looks like the march-past of a glistening army.

Isaiah's faith, communicated to Hezekiah, was vindicated, and the Assyrian army rolled south to be decimated by their visitation of plague (4-8).

   Half unable to believe such a vast deliverance, the people go out, walk with new wonder round their undamaged walls (12, 13), but reverently note that it is what dwells within that gives salvation (1, 3, 14). So with the City of Mansoul, as Bunyan called it. It is God who occupies the hidden sanctuary who makes life's ramparts stand.

49 WORDS OF WISDOM

Hear this all you peoples;
  listen, all who live in this world,
²both low and high,
  rich and poor alike:
³my mouth will speak words of wisdom;
  tne utterance from my heart will give
    understanding.
⁴I will turn my ear to a proverb;
  with the harp I will expound my riddle:

⁵Why should I fear when evil days come,
  when wicked deceivers surround me—
⁶those who trust in their wealth
  and boast of their great riches?
⁷No man can redeem the life of another
  or give to God a ransom for him—
⁸the ransom for a life is costly,
  no payment is ever enough—
⁹that he should live on for ever and not see
    decay.

¹⁰For all can see that wise men die;
  the foolish and the senseless alike
    perish
  and leave their wealth to others.
¹¹Their tombs will remain their houses for
    ever,
  their dwellings for endless generations,
  though they had named lands after
    themselves.

¹²But man, despite his riches, does not
    endure;
  he is like the beasts that perish.

¹³This is the fate of those who trust in
    themselves,
  and of their followers, who approve their
    sayings.   Selah
¹⁴Like sheep they are destined for the
    grave,
  and death will feed on them.
The upright will rule over them in the
    morning;
  their forms will decay in the grave
  far from their princely mansions.
¹⁵But God will redeem my soul from the
    grave;
  he will surely take me to
    himself.   Selah

¹⁶Do not be overawed when a man grows
    rich,
  when the splendour of his house
    increases;
¹⁷For he will take nothing with him when
    he dies,
  his splendour will not descend with him.
¹⁸Though while he lived he counted himself
    blessed—
  and men praise you when you
    prosper—
¹⁹he will join the generation of his fathers,
  who will never see the light of life.

²⁰A man who has riches without
    understanding
  is like the beasts that perish.

*This solemn theme, the pathetic fragility of
life, and the awesome equality of death
has preoccupied the poetry of the world
from Babylon's epic of Gilgamesh to
Tennyson's In Memoriam and Housman's
polished verse.*

*Nothing avails. 'The old wind, in the old
anger sweeps all away', rich, poor, great,
small. 'The paths of glory lead but to the
grave.'*

*But pause on verse 15. It is too commonly
said that the Old Testament had no
conception of another life. More than once
some startling thought like this intrudes.
The poet of this psalm could see no logic
in a grisly event which levelled good and
bad in the awful dissolution of the grave.
He suddenly thought of Enoch (Genesis
5.14), and he uses the same verb in his
momentary reaching after resurrection
(15).*

*The psalm ends with the sentiments
which conclude Psalm 37. For the bad,
death, to be sure. Such men are beasts (20).
The good can be calm (16), but the
psalmist seems to have glimpsed
something more. We have an empty tomb.*

50 JUDGMENT

The Mighty One, God, the LORD,
  speaks and summons the earth
from the rising of the sun to the place
    where it sets.
² From Zion, perfect in beauty, God shines
    forth.
³ Our God comes and will not be silent;
  a fire devours before him,
  and around him a tempest rages.
⁴ He summons the heavens above,
    and the earth, that he may judge his
    people:
⁵ 'Gather to me my consecrated ones,
    who made a covenant with me by
    sacrifice.'
⁶ And the heavens proclaim his
    righteousness,
  for God himself is judge.   *Selah*

⁷ 'Hear, O my people, and I will speak,
    O Israel, and I will testify against you:
    I am God, your God.
⁸ I do not rebuke you for your sacrifices
    or your burnt offerings, which are ever
      before me.
⁹ I have no need of a bull from your stall
    or of goats from your pens,
¹⁰ for every animal of the forest is mine,
    and cattle on a thousand hills.
¹¹ I know every bird in the mountains,
    and the creatures of the field are mine.
¹² If I were hungry I would not tell you,
    for the world is mine, and all that is in it.
¹³ Do I eat the flesh of bulls
    or drink the blood of goats?
¹⁴ Sacrifice thank-offerings to God,
    fulfil your vows to the Most High,

¹⁵and call upon me in the day of trouble;
  I will deliver you, and you will honour
  me.'
¹⁶But to the wicked, God says:

'What right have you to recite my laws
  or take my covenant on your lips?
¹⁷You hate my instruction
  and cast my words behind you.
¹⁸When you see a thief, you join with him;
  you throw in your lot with adulterers.
¹⁹You use your mouth for evil
  and harness your tongue to deceit.
²⁰You speak continually against your
  brother
  and slander your own mother's son.

²¹These things you have done and I kept
  silent;
  you thought I was altogether like you.
But I will rebuke you
  and accuse you to your face.

²²'Consider this, you who forget God,
  or I will tear you to pieces, with none to
  rescue:
²³he who sacrifices thank-offerings honours
  me,
  and he prepares the way
  so that I may show him the salvation of
  God.'

Asaph, to whom this psalm is attributed, seems to have been the founder of a musicians' guild in David's day, which endured for centuries. Any 'Asaph psalm' could be from any member, and so could fit a wide range of dates.

This stern word against formalism, that blight on all ordered worship, was a theme of many prophets——Amos, Isaiah, Hosea, Jeremiah, Micah, Zechariah. It could belong to Hezekiah's revival.

'Hear, O Israel,' the Shema (Deuteronomy 6.4, 5), startles Israel to attention (7). It is as pagan to turn God's law to formality, as it is to know no law of God. Sacrifice and ritual had (and have) value only in so far as they reflect an attitude of heart.

Man dare not treat God as if he were mere man to be flattered, served fitfully and faithlessly as if he could be mocked (21). It all has a final test and that lies in the consideration of what profession does to the way a man lives (23).

51 REPENTANCE

Have mercy on me, O God,
according to your unfailing love;
according to your great compassion
blot out my transgressions.
²Wash away all my iniquity
and cleanse me from my sin.

³For I know my transgressions,
and my sin is always before me.
⁴Against you, you only, have I sinned
and done what is evil in your sight,
so that you are proved right when you
speak
and justified when you judge.
⁵Surely I have been a sinner from birth,
sinful from the time my mother
conceived me.
⁶Surely you desire truth in the inner parts;
you teach me wisdom in the inmost
place.

⁷Cleanse me with hyssop, and I shall be
clean;
wash me, and I shall be whiter than
snow.
⁸Let me hear joy and gladness;
let the bones you have crushed rejoice.
⁹Hide your face from my sins
and blot out all my iniquity.

¹⁰Create in me a pure heart, O God,
and renew a steadfast spirit within me.
¹¹Do not cast me from your presence
or take your Holy Spirit from me.
¹²Restore to me the joy of your salvation
and grant me a willing spirit, to sustain
me.

¹³Then I will teach transgressors your ways,
and sinners will turn back to you.
¹⁴Save me from bloodguiltiness, O God,
the God who saves me,
and my tongue will sing of your
righteousness.
¹⁵O Lord, open my lips,
and my mouth will declare your praise.
¹⁶You do not delight in sacrifice or I would
bring it;
you do not take pleasure in burnt
offerings.

¹⁷The sacrifices of God are a broken spirit;
a broken and contrite heart,
O God, you will not despise.

¹⁸In your good pleasure make Zion prosper;
build up the walls of Jerusalem.
¹⁹Then there will be righteous sacrifices,
whole burnt offerings to delight you;
then bulls will be offered on your altar.

*There can be no sane denial of the dark
background of this most harrowing and
heart-searching of the penitential psalms.
Stabbed to final awareness of the
beginnings of his shocking sin by Nathan's
brave act (2 Samuel) 11.2-12.14), and the
reality of the heart's decay (6, 10), David
made no attempt to shield himself.*

*He wrote this confession. He probably
stood, bowed in grief, while the Levites
sang it aloud. It is possible to see
splendour in his penitence. His heart is
wide open to God's agonising thrust, and
in utter openness he surrenders the whole
fearsome clutter of evil to God.*

*Anything thus surrendered to such
creative hands can be taken and
transmuted into good. And so it comes
about that a cruel murder and a base
adultery became a prayer for every sinner.
And how many millions have found the
path to washing and forgiveness in the
soul-scouring words of this noble prayer of
penitence? (End at verse 17. The last two
verses were a Levite's addition after
Jerusalem was destroyed and not part of
David's prayer.)*

52 LIKE AN OLIVE TREE

Why do you boast of evil, you
mighty man?
Why do you boast all day long,
you who are a disgrace in the eyes of
God?
²Your tongue plots destruction;
it is like a sharpened razor,
you who practise deceit.
³You love evil rather than good,
falsehood rather than speaking the
truth.   *Selah*
⁴You love every harmful word,
O you deceitful tongue!

⁵Surely God will bring you down to
everlasting ruin;
he will snatch you up and tear you from
your tent;
he will uproot you from the land of the
living.   *Selah*
⁶The righteous will see and fear;
they will laugh at him, saying,
⁷'Here now is the man
who did not make God his stronghold
but trusted in his great wealth
and grew strong by destroying others!'

⁸But I am like an olive tree
flourishing in the house of God;
I trust in God's unfailing love
for ever and ever.
⁹I will praise you for ever for what you have
done;
in your name I will hope, for your name
is good.
I will praise you in the presence of your
saints.

*It is a loathsome experience to meet lies
and treachery. It is a far too familiar
experience. David had been helped by the
priest of Nob. Doeg, the Edomite, Saul's
chief herdsman, had informed, and death
fell on an innocent community, the situation
traditionally associated with this psalm.*

*Hence this formal curse, and verses 1 to
5 were probably sent to Doeg. A formal
communication was a terrible weapon and
could destroy its object. It is still a
powerful force in the mind of desert
Bedouin and among many primitive tribes.*

*Then, as though to cleanse his mind of
words so devastating, David passes to the
lovely figure of the olive. The olive ever
springs again from roots almost beyond
destruction, a living symbol of vitality. It is
a valiant tree, bearing its best fruit when
mature. It thrives best in soil hostile to
other trees, and it provides essential food
in some economies today, a tree of
beneficence, enduring strength and hope.*

53 THE SONS OF MEN

The fool says in his heart,
  'There is no God.'
They are corrupt, and their ways are vile;
  there is no one who does good.

²God looks down from heaven on the sons
    of men
  to see if there are any who understand,
    any who seek God.
³Everyone has turned away,
  they have together become corrupt;
there is no one who does good,
    not even one.

⁴Will the evildoers never learn–
    those who devour my people as men eat
      bread
    and who do not call on God?
⁵There they were, overwhelmed with
    dread,
  where there was nothing to dread.
God scattered the bones of those who
    attacked you;
  you put them to shame, for God
    despised them.

⁶Oh, that salvation for Israel would come
    out of Zion!
  When God restores the fortunes of his
    people,
  let Jacob rejoice and Israel be glad!

For some reason beyond recovery or guess, the compiler repeated Psalm 14 here with slight changes in verses 5 and 6. And verse 5 suggests that this version could be an old Davidic psalm revived for worship after the destruction of Sennacherib. Such deliverance confounded doubt. There was a God indeed, and he cared and had most notably intervened.

54 GOD MY HELP

Save me, O God, by your name;
  vindicate me by your might.
²Hear my prayer, O God;
  listen to the words of my mouth.

³Strangers are attacking me;
  ruthless men seek my life —
  men without regard for God.   *Selah*

⁴Surely God is my help;
  the Lord is the one who sustains me.

⁵Let evil recoil on those who slander me;
  in your faithfulness destroy them.

⁶I will sacrifice a freewill offering to you;
  I will praise your name, O LORD,
  for it is good.
⁷For he has delivered me from all my
  troubles,
  and my eyes have looked in triumph on
  my foes.

*To be betrayed by Doeg, the Edomite was
for David a dark enough experience. It was
the crowning bitterness to find his own
people, in a village he had himself
delivered from a Philistine raid, also turn
on him. Saul's savage reprisals against all
who aided David's six hundred guerrillas
were paying dividends.*

*Godless and 'ruthless', the men of Keilah
were anxious to be rid of David's presence
in their territory. He turned to God, as he
always did in these days of trouble. He did
not realise that they were to prove the
greatest days in his life. God taught him in
the darkness what eluded him in the light.*

*And so treachery made this little pearl of
prayer for days of peril. Sir Jacob Astley
prayed before the Battle of Edgehill: 'Lord,
Thou knowest how busy I must be this day.
If I forget Thee, do not Thou forget me.'*

55 IN DESOLATION

Listen to my prayer, O God,
  do not ignore my plea;
² hear me and answer me.
  My thoughts trouble me and I am
      distraught
³ at the voice of the enemy,
    at the stares of the wicked;
  for they bring down suffering upon me
    and revile me in their anger.

⁴My heart is in anguish within me;
    the terrors of death assail me.
⁵Fear and trembling have beset me;
    horror has overwhelmed me.
⁶I said, 'Oh, that I had the wings of a dove!
    I would fly away and be at rest –
⁷I would flee far away
    and stay in the desert;   *Selah*
⁸I would hurry to my place of shelter,

far from the tempest and storm.

9Confuse the wicked, O Lord, confound
      their speech,
   for I see violence and strife in the city.
10Day and night they prowl about on its
      walls;
   malice and abuse are within it.
11Destructive forces are at work in the city;
   threats and lies never leave its streets.

12If an enemy were insulting me,
   I could endure it;
 if a foe were raising himself against me,
   I could hide from him.
13But it is you, a man like myself,
   my companion, my close friend,
14with whom I enjoyed sweet fellowship
   as we walked with the throng at the
      house of God.

15Let death take my enemies by surprise;
   let them go down alive to the grave,
   for evil finds lodging among them.
16But I call to God, and the LORD saves me.
17Evening, morning and noon I cry out in
      distress,
   and he hears my voice.
18He ransoms me unharmed
   from the battle waged against me,
   even though many oppose me.
19God, who is enthroned for ever,
   will hear them and afflict
      them–   Selah
 men who never change their ways
   and have no fear of God.

20My companion attacks his friends;
   he violates his covenant.
21His speech is smooth as butter,
   yet war is in his heart;
 his words are more soothing than oil,
   yet they are drawn swords.

22Cast your cares on the LORD
   and he will sustain you;
   he will never let the righteous fall.

23But you, O God, will bring down the
      wicked
   into the pit of corruption;
 bloodthirsty and deceitful men
   will not live out half their days.

But as for me, I trust in you.

*This surely is a psalm from the same
period as Psalm 2. Screened by a
sycophantic court from reality, David, in
sudden shock, realises he is hated. In
desperation he turns to God, and certainly,
a God who commanded man not to turn
away from another's trouble, would, he
knew, not turn from him (1; Deuteronomy
22.1-4).*

*It was a desperate situation (2-5), and the
thought of retreat to the wilderness is
already taking shape (6-8). So fled Elijah, so
Moses. The desert was Israel's place of
beginning, and it is good, in time of stress,
to retreat to the first source of our strength.*

*It is clear that Absalom was not alone. A
conspiracy had been afoot led by one who
had been a trusted friend. Perhaps
Ahitophel was the Judas of the hour, and
it has been suggested that he was related
to the enigmatic Bathsheba, of whose
repentance there is no record. With hot
and vehement beginnings (12-15), the
prayer quietens. It is part of prayer's
purpose to calm the spirit. Peter picked up
verse 22 in a day of looming trouble.
(1 Peter 5.7).*

56 SLANDERERS

Be merciful to me, O God, for men
hotly pursue me;
all day long they press their attack.
[2] My slanderers pursue me all day long;
many are attacking me in their pride.

[3] When I am afraid,
I will trust in you.
[4] In God, whose word I praise,
in God I trust; I will not be afraid.
What can mortal man do to me?

[5] All day long they twist my words;
they are always plotting to harm me.
[6] They conspire, they lurk,
they watch my steps,
eager to take my life.

[7] On no account let them escape;
in your anger, O God, bring down the
nations.
[8] Record my lament;
list my tears on your scroll–
are they not in your record?

[9] Then my enemies will turn back
when I call for help.
By this I will know that God is for me.

¹⁰In God, whose word I praise,
  in the LORD, whose word I praise–
¹¹ In God I trust; I will not be afraid.
  What can man do to me?

¹²I am under vows to you, O God;
  I will present my thank-offerings to you.
¹³For you have delivered my soul from
      death
  and my feet from stumbling,
 that I may walk before God
   in the light of life.

The title suggests that David was a prisoner in Gath, town of his old enemy Goliath. Or was it the occasion of his shameful defection? It was a time of great danger, in any case (1), and it called for prayer (3). Fear is faith's testing. The Philistines could have killed him, and our generation, accustomed to 'brain-washing', should not find their form of torment difficult to believe (4-6). Against such devilry, a 'steadfast mind', trusting in God—(Isaiah 26.3) is the strongest defence (7). That determination sets the mood for the rest of the psalm, with a splendid climax in verse 13. It should be the Christian's daily prayer.

57 IN DANGER

Have mercy on me, O God, have
mercy on me,
for in you my soul takes refuge.
I will take refuge in the shadow of your
wings
until the disaster has passed.

²I cry out to God Most High,
to God, who fulfils his purpose for me.
³He sends from heaven and saves me,
rebuking those who hotly pursue
me;   *Selah*
God sends his love and his faithfulness.

⁴I am in the midst of lions;
I lie among ravenous beasts —
men whose teeth are spears and arrows,
whose tongues are sharp swords.

⁵Be exalted, O God, above the heavens;
let your glory be over all the earth.

⁶They spread a net for my feet —
I was bowed down in distress.
They dug a pit in my path —
but they have fallen into it
themselves.   *Selah*

⁷My heart is steadfast, O God,
my heart is steadfast;
I will sing and make music.

⁸Awake, harp and lyre!
I will awaken the dawn.

⁹I will praise you, O Lord, among the
nations;
I will sing of you among the peoples.
¹⁰For great is your love, reaching to the
heavens;
your faithfulness reaches to the skies.

¹¹Be exalted, O God, above the heavens;
let your glory be over all the earth.

Was an escape from Gath to the cave-fill
wilderness the occasion of this psalm?
Better be hunted by Saul's swordsmen th
tormented by the Philistines. There is qu
trust now, however perilous the past.
Physical danger is simpler to meet than
peril in the soul, and this psalm is the
utterance of a heart at rest. The sharpest
note of pain is in verse 4, where the old

evil of slander, which David always found difficult to bear, is alive again. In the star-strewn desert night of Psalm 8, David sees the might of God (5) and the doom of earthly evil (6). His song stirs the very dawn (8). He is free from the night's peril, and morning comes with peace that fills the very sky (8, 10). The closing verses are pure worship, David at his cleanest, the poet at his best.

58 WICKED RULERS

Do rulers indeed speak justly?
Do you judge uprightly among men?
2 No, in your heart you devise injustice,
and your hands mete out violence on the earth.
3 Even from birth the wicked go astray;
from the womb they are wayward and speak lies.
4 Their venom is like the venom of a snake,
like that of a cobra that has stopped its ears,
5 that will not heed the tune of the charmer,
however skilful the enchanter may be.

6 Break the teeth in their mouths, O God;
tear out, O LORD, the fangs of the lions!
7 Let them vanish like water that flows away;
when they draw the bow, let their arrows be blunted.
8 Like a slug melting away as it moves along,
like a stillborn child, may they not see the sun.

Psalms of trouble and stress are gathered in this part of the book. Hence this fierce little protest against the injustice and tyranny into which Saul's Israel had sunk. 'Do you, indeed, decree justice, you sovereign rulers?' the first verse should run, as R.K. Harrison translates. Rulers bear a heavy burden, they frequently fail (2). Nothing can emerge clean from a personality which harbours evil at its core. Such judges are like serpents, bent from birth (3-5), and carrying their poison within.

With verse 6 we have again the language of vengeance. The power of words was more deeply felt in ancient times, and such blazing speech could fall like God's arrows on those who deserved such wounding. Christ himself condemned hypocrisy in speech. Hence the terrible imagery to which the helpless psalmist was driven (10). Who does not crave for God's vindication of good? It is a strong call to faith (11).

59 A PRAYER FOR HELP

Deliver me from my enemies, O
   God;
   protect me from those who rise up
      against me.
²Deliver me from evildoers
   and save me from bloodthirsty men.

³See how they lie in wait for me!
   Fierce men conspire against me
   for no offence or sin of mine, O LORD.
⁴I have done no wrong, yet they are ready
      to attack me.
   Arise to help me; look on my plight!
⁵O LORD God Almighty, the God of Israel,
   rouse yourself to punish all the nations;
   show no mercy to wicked
      traitors.   *Selah*

⁶They return at evening,
   snarling like dogs,
   and prowl about the city.
⁷See what they spew from their mouths —
   they spew out swords from their lips,
   and they say, 'Who can hear us?'
⁸But you, O LORD, laugh at them;
   you scoff at all those nations.

⁹O my Strength, I watch for you;
   you, O God, are my fortress
¹⁰   my loving God will go before me and
   will let me gloat over those who slander
      me.
¹¹But do not kill them, O Lord our shield,
   or my people will forget.
In your might make them wander about,
   and bring them down.
¹²For the sins of their mouths,
   for the words of their lips,
   let them be caught in their pride.
For the curses and lies they utter,
¹³   consume them in wrath,
   consume them till they are no more.
Then it will be known to the ends of the
      earth
   that God rules over Jacob.   *Selah*

¹⁴They return at evening,
   snarling like dogs,
   and prowl about the city.

¹⁵They wander about for food
   and howl if not satisfied.
¹⁶But I will sing of your strength,
   in the morning I will sing of your love;
for you are my fortress,
   my refuge in times of trouble.
¹⁷O my Strength, I sing praise to you;
   you, O God, are my fortress, my loving
      God.

*This psalm clearly refers to the same
period of trouble as Psalm 58. It need not,
of course, have been written at the time of
danger (1 Samuel 19.11-18), when Saul's
daughter served David well. Poetry, said
Wordsworth, is 'emotion recollected in
tranquility', and the quieter psalms of
danger illustrate his words. Saul, like all
tyrants, had his secret agents, and had to
move carefully against a popular hero.*

*Hence a certain confidence. Warily but
calmly, David sees the prowling assassins
and the slanderers about their work, and
invokes God's vengeance on them.
Perhaps the morning of deliverance has
come (16). Perhaps he is back, a king now,
in the place of old peril. Perhaps the tools
of Saul's evil are still alive, bearing in fear,
their shame (11, 14, 15). It was 'mercy
all . . .*

60 A PRAYER FOR VICTORY

You have rejected us, O God, and
burst forth upon us;
   you have been angry—now restore us!
²You have shaken the land and torn it open;
   mend its fractures, for it is quaking.
³You have shown your people desperate
      times;
   you have given us wine that makes us
      stagger.

⁴But for those who fear you, you have raised
      a banner
   to be unfurled against the
      bow.   *Selah*
⁵Save us and help us with your right hand,
   that those you love may be delivered.

⁶God has spoken from his sanctuary:
   'In triumph I will parcel out Shechem
   and measure off the Valley of Succoth.
⁷Gilead is mine, and Manasseh is mine;
   Ephraim is my helmet, Judah my
      sceptre.
⁸Moab is my washbasin,
   upon Edom I toss my sandal;
   over Philistia I shout in triumph.'

⁹Who will bring me to the fortified city?
   Who will lead me to Edom?
¹⁰It is not you, O God, who have rejected
      us
   and no longer go out with our armies?
¹¹Give us aid against our enemy,
   for the help of man is worthless.
¹²With God we shall gain the victory,
   and he will trample down our enemies.

*Israel's frontiers have never been quiet.
The Old Testament was written behind
walls of fear. David set himself to find
secure lines and it was under him that
Israel came nearest to winning secure
borders. He seems to have been forced to
abandon a northern drive (2 Samuel 8) to
turn and deal with an attack from Edom
and a restive Philistia. Joab's column had
rushed south, and David is shaken by near
disaster, and throws himself on God.*

*Perhaps some fault or weakness had
betrayed him (1, 2), and God wished to
teach a needed lesson. He sometimes uses
circumstances to achieve his ends (3). It is
well to be alert for such instruction.*

*Confidence returns with verse 8. With
God's help Moab is no more than a basin*
*which a guest's feet are washed, Edom
merely a servant to whom his shoes are
thrown, Philistia the people of fallen
Goliath. Failure is not final, and there is
always a banner to show where the king
stands.*

61 A STRONG TOWER

Hear my cry, O God;
  listen to my prayer.
[2] From the ends of the earth I call to you,
  I call as my heart grows faint;
  lead me to the rock that is higher than I.

[3] For you have been my refuge,
  a strong tower against the foe.

[4] I long to dwell in your tent for ever
  and take refuge in the shelter of your
    wings.   *Selah*
[5] For you have heard my vows, O God;
  you have given me the heritage of those
    who fear your name.

[6] Increase the days of the king's life,
  his years for many generations.
[7] May he be enthroned in God's presence
    for ever;
  appoint your love and faithfulness to
    protect him.

[8] Then will I ever sing praise to your name
  and fulfil my vows day after day.

*Good news, perhaps, has come from Joab.
For one driving hard on campaign towards
Joshua's boundary of the Euphrates (1, 4),
the far north might seem 'the ends of the
earth' (2). It is illuminating to see the
imagery of the Bible in the context of time
and place. In those lands a rock is always
merciful shade from the burning sun, and
there are many fortress crags like Masada
(3). David's eyes were always alert for a
defensive position, now that he had risked
leaving himself with an inadequate army
by sending Joab south. The landscape itself
would have to serve them, and God's sky
give the helpless cover, like a chieftain's
inviolate tent, or the eagle, wings spread
over its nest.*

*Perhaps the last three verses were
added by the 'choirmaster' to the royal
psalm to make a 'national anthem'. This in
no way diminishes the authority of the
psalm. Indeed, the words are culled from
David's own poems.*

62 GOD ALONE

My soul finds rest in God alone;
my salvation comes from him.
²He alone is my rock and my salvation;
he is my fortress, I shall never be
shaken.

³How long will you assault a man?
Would all of you throw him down–
this leaning wall, this tottering fence?
⁴They fully intend to topple him
from his lofty place;
they take delight in lies.
With their mouths they bless,
but in their hearts they curse.   *Selah*

⁵Find rest, O my soul, in God alone;
my hope comes from him.
⁶He alone is my rock and my salvation;
he is my fortress, I shall not be shaken.
⁷My salvation and my honour depend on
God;
he is my mighty rock, my refuge.
⁸Trust in him at all times, O people;
pour out your hearts to him,
for God is our refuge.   *Selah*

⁹Lowborn men are but a breath,
the highborn are but a lie;
if weighed on a balance, they are nothing;
together they are only a breath.
¹⁰Do not trust in extortion
or take pride in stolen goods;
though your riches increase,
do not set your heart on them.
¹¹One thing God has spoken,
two things have I heard:
that you, O God, are strong,
¹²and that you, O Lord, are loving.
Surely you will reward each person
according to what he has done.

The theme of the rock and the refuge is picked up and expanded. Psalms 42-72 have much to say of the storms of David's life, and this piece is a summary. Perhaps, too, if the compiler was a rabbi of the exiled Jews, such psalms of refuge were previous and intimate utterances.

Moffatt makes the psalm begin movingly: 'Leave it all quietly to God, my soul.' In such faith, feet firm on the rock, a man can turn to face an evil assault (3, 4). A leader is never secure, but faithful leaders can stand confidently in the knowledge that they do not stand alone (5-8). He gives what no trust in men can give (9), nor any material acquisition, dishonestly or honestly acquired (10).

This, says David, is 'the great, repeated lesson of life', that strength (10) mercy and justice (12) have, in this world, only one source—God.

63 LONGING FOR GOD

O God, you are my God,
  earnestly I seek you;
my soul thirsts for you,
  my body longs for you,
in a dry and weary land
  where there is no water.

²I have seen you in the sanctuary
  and beheld your power and your glory.
³Because your love is better than life,
  my lips will glorify you.
⁴I will praise you as long as I live,
  and in your name I will lift up my hands.
⁵My soul will be satisfied as with the
    richest of foods;
  with singing lips my mouth will praise
    you.

⁶On my bed I remember you;
  I think of you through the watches of the
    night.
⁷Because you are my help,
  I sing in the shadow of your wings.
⁸I stay close to you;
  your right hand upholds me.

⁹They who seek my life will be destroyed;
  they will go down to the depths of the
    earth.
¹⁰They will be given over to the sword
  and become food for jackals.

¹¹But the king will rejoice in God;
  all who swear by God's name will praise
    him,
  while the mouths of liars will be
    silenced.

It is impossible to date this song of the 'wilderness', but, whether it came from the days of Saul's persecution or Absalom's treachery, it is a hymn of quiet trust and deep tranquility.

It is only those who thirst after righteousness who find it (Matthew 5.6) and thirst must be imagined as they alone know it, who live in a sun-scorched, arid land (1). With such fierce desire David longed for God, and his satisfying love (2, 3). Five exquisite verses of pure worship follow. How few know God in this way—a presence completely possessing the being, filling the silent night (5, 6), shadowing, protecting (7), a guide to whose hand a man may cling (8). The eagle, floating high with outspread wings, was a common sight in the wilderness (Psalm 17.8; 36.7; 57.1) and a ready symbol for the all-seeing, the wide-ranging, steadfastly commanding God. If this is a psalm of Absalom's day, it stands nearer to Psalm 23 than Psalm 6. The valley is past. Victory is in the king's hand.

64 ENEMIES

Hear me, O God, as I voice my complaint;
protect my life from the threat of the enemy.

[2] Hide me from the conspiracy of the wicked,
from that noisy crowd of evildoers,
[3] who sharpen their tongues like swords
and aim their words like deadly arrows.
[4] They shoot from ambush at the innocent man;
they shoot at him suddenly, without fear.

[5] They encourage each other in evil plans,
they talk about hiding their snares;
they say, 'Who will see them?'
[6] They plot injustice and say,
'We have devised a perfect plan!'
Surely the mind and heart of man are cunning.

[7] But God will shoot them with arrows;
suddenly they will be struck down.
[8] He will turn their own tongues against them
and bring them to ruin;
all who see them will shake their heads in scorn.
[9] All mankind will fear;
they will proclaim the works of God
and ponder what he has done.

[10] Let the righteous rejoice in the LORD
and take refuge in him;
let all the upright in heart praise him!

The events behind this psalm have been seen in one shape or another through a group of psalms going back to Psalm 52. A common theme has been God in time of trouble. They have much to say to all who find the path bent and rough.

The complaint is the common one—conspiracy and the war of slander. Vilification prepares the way for revolt. There has been a battle for men's minds, and evil has won some victories. Words can be arrows and the ancient bow was a formidable weapon, capable, as the Assyrian frescoes show, of smashing a lion's back with a shaft. So powerfully have wickedly aimed words sped (3-6).

At last the arrow of retribution speeds, (7), so aimed that none can doubt what bow sent it on its way. David craved such vindication, not for himself only, but for God and God's righteous people (9, 10).

65 GOD'S HARVEST

Praise awaits you, O God, in Zion;
to you our vows will be fulfilled.
²O you who hear prayer,
to you all men will come.
³When we were overwhelmed by sins,
you atoned for our transgressions.
⁴Blessed is the man you choose
and bring near to live in your courts!
We are filled with the good things of your
house,
of your holy temple.
⁵You answer us with awesome deeds of
righteousness,
O God our Saviour,
the hope of all the ends of the earth
and of the farthest seas,
⁶who formed the mountains by your power,
having armed yourself with strength,
⁷who stilled the roaring of the seas,
the roaring of their waves,
and the turmoil of the nations.
⁸Those living far away fear your wonders;
where morning dawns and evening
fades
you call forth songs of joy.

⁹You care for the land and water it;
you enrich it abundantly.
The streams of God are filled with water
to provide the people with grain,
for so you have ordained it.
¹⁰You drench its furrows
and level its ridges;
you soften it with showers
and bless its crops.
¹¹You crown the year with your bounty,
and your carts overflow with abundance.
¹²The grasslands of the desert overflow;
the hills are clothed with gladness.
¹³The meadows are covered with flocks
and the valleys are mantled with grain;
they shout for joy and sing.

Were it not for the traditional ascription of this psalm to David, it might have been tempting to name Isaiah as the author. Perhaps the great prophet overwrote a Davidic psalm. Observe Isaiah's universal gospel in verses 2 and 5.

What impresses most in this beautiful hymn is the enormous gap it reveals between Israel's conception of the creator and sustainer of all life, and the fertility gods of Canaan, the obscene rituals which prompted such mythological creations to inseminate the fields, and the crudities of all neighbouring theologies.

Note the 'Christian' maturity of verse 3, which links with such immediate instancy the confession of sin with forgiveness granted, and the majesty of the God who stills the sea and human tumult (7; Mark 4.39), and yet is known and visible to man, as Paul told the countrymen of Lystra (Acts 14.17), in the beneficence of his hands. The theme is often taken up in later psalms.

66 SING TO GOD

Shout with joy to God, all the earth!
2 Sing to the glory of his name;
offer him glory and praise!
3 Say to God, 'How awesome are your deeds!
So great is your power
that your enemies cringe before you.
4 All the earth bows down to you;
they sing praise to you,
they sing praise to your
name.'   *Selah*

5 Come and see what God has done,
how awesome his works in man's behalf!
6 He turned the sea into dry land,
they passed through the river on foot—
come, let us rejoice in him.
7 He rules for ever by his power,
his eyes watch the nations—
let not the rebellious rise up against
him.   *Selah*

8 Praise our God, O peoples,
let the sound of his praise be heard;
9 he has preserved our lives
and kept our feet from slipping.
10 For you, O God, tested us;
you refined us like silver.
11 You brought us into prison
and laid burdens on our backs.
12 You let men ride over our heads;
we went through fire and water,
but you brought us to a place of
abundance.

13 I will come to your temple with burnt
offerings
and fulfil my vows to you—
14 vows my lips promised and my mouth
spoke
when I was in trouble.
15 I will sacrifice fat animals to you
and an offering of rams;
I will offer bulls and goats.   *Selah*

16 Come and listen, all you who fear God;
let me tell you what he has done for me.
17 I cried out to him with my mouth;
his praise was on my tongue.
18 If I had cherished sin in my heart,
the Lord would not have listened;
19 but God has surely listened
and heard my voice in prayer.
20 Praise be to God,
who has not rejected my prayer
or withheld his love from me!

Echoes of Psalm 65 perhaps led to this psalm of unknown authorship being located here. A central section (8-12) suggests that there had been some vast deliverance. They stand where they might well have fallen (9), tested; they have been proved gleaming silver (10), they have richly survived the overwhelming foe (12).

The writer resumes in the first person, or else writes in the first person that each man may take and make the words his own (13-15). In that art lies the pattern for all public prayer. The closing verses are pure gold, and full of the true meaning of prayer. Prayer must proceed from a heart which desires purity. God does not demand perfection or none could pray. He does ask for a contrite heart, where no fetid corner is deliberately screened from him.

67 THE NATIONS PRAISE

May God be gracious to us and
bless us
and make his face to shine upon
us; *Selah*
²may your ways be known on earth,
your salvation among all nations.

³May the peoples praise you, O God;
may all the peoples praise you.
⁴May the nations be glad and sing for joy,
for you rule the peoples justly
and guide the nations of the
earth. *Selah*
⁵May the peoples praise you, O God;
may all the peoples praise you.

⁶Then the land will yield its harvest,
and God, our God, will bless us.
⁷God will bless us,
and all the ends of the earth will fear
him.

*This small hymn of peace is based on the
benediction of Numbers 6.24-27. The
concept of a God of all the earth is as old
as the Covenant with Abraham, whose
posterity was as the sand and the stars. It is
a noble thought embedded in the Old
Testament, and was no less than the final
mission of Israel.*

*Health could come to a sick world (2)
today if Christ could but be universally
accepted, and all nations be united to
praise God (3). The spectacle of God as
guide and judge is an exalted one (4), and
touches the psalm with warmth. Such
Hebrew thought, the vision of a God of
'loving kindness and tender mercy',
reaches out towards God in Christ, and the
message of the Christian gospel.
Aspirations stand on the very edge of
prophecy.*

68 A FATHER TO THE FATHERLESS

May God arise, may his enemies
  be scattered;
  may his foes flee before him.
2 As smoke is blown away by the wind,
  may you blow them away;
as wax melts before the fire,
  may the wicked perish before God.
3 But may the righteous be glad
  and rejoice before God;
  may they be happy and joyful.

4 Sing to God, sing praise to his name,
  extol him who rides on the clouds–
his name is the LORD–
  and rejoice before him.
5 A father to the fatherless, a defender of
  widows,
  is God in his holy dwelling.
6 God sets the lonely in families,
  he leads forth the prisoners with singing;
  but the rebellious live in a sun-scorched
  land.

7 When you went out before your people, O
  God,
  when you marched through the
  wasteland,   Selah
8 the earth shook,
  the heavens poured down rain,
  before God, the One of Sinai,
  before God, the God of Israel.
9 You gave abundant showers, O God;
  you refreshed your weary inheritance.
10 Your people settled in it,
  and from your bounty, O God, you
  provided for the poor.

11 The Lord announced the word,
  and great was the company of those who
  proclaimed it:
12 'Kings and armies flee in haste;
in the camps men divide the plunder.
13 Even while you sleep among the
  campfires,
  the wings of my dove are sheathed with
  silver,
its feathers with shining gold.'
14 When the Almighty scattered the kings in
  the land,
  it was like snow fallen on Zalmon.

15 The mountains of Bashan are majestic
  mountains;
  rugged are the mountains of Bashan.
16 Why gaze in envy, O rugged mountains,
  at the mountain where God chooses to
  reign,
  where the LORD himself will dwell for
  ever?
17 The chariots of God are tens of thousands
  and thousands of thousands:
  the Lord has come from Sinai into his
  sanctuary.
18 When you ascended on high,
  you led captives in your train;
  you received gifts from men.
  even from the rebellious–
  that you, O LORD God, might dwell there.
19 Praise be to the Lord, to God our Saviour,
  who daily bears our burdens.   Selah
20 Our God is a God who saves;
  from the Sovereign LORD comes escape
  from death.

21 Surely God will crush the heads of his
  enemies,
  the hairy crowns of those who go on in
  their sins.
22 The Lord says, 'I will bring you from
  Bashan;
  I will bring you from the depths of the
  sea,
23 that you may plunge your feet in the blood
  of your foes,
  while the tongues of your dogs have
  their share.'

24 Your procession has come into view, O
  God,
  the procession of my God and King into
  the sanctuary.
25 In front are the singers, after them the
  musicians;
  with them are the maidens playing
  tambourines.
26 Praise God in the great congregation;
  praise the LORD in the assembly of
  Israel.

²⁷There is the little tribe of Benjamin,
    leading them,
  there the great throng of Judah's princes,
  and there the princes of Zebulun and of
    Naphtali.

²⁸Summon your power, O God;
  show us your strength, O God, as you
    have done before.

²⁹Because of your temple at Jerusalem
  kings will bring you gifts.
³⁰Rebuke the beast among the reeds,
  the herd of bulls among the calves of the
    nations.
 Humbled, may it bring bars of silver.
  Scatter the nations who delight in war.
³¹Envoys will come from Egypt;
  Cush will submit herself to God.

³²Sing to God, O kingdoms of the earth,
   sing praise to the Lord,   *Selah*
³²to him who rides the ancient skies above,
   who thunders with mighty voice.
³⁴Proclaim the power of God,
   whose majesty is over Israel,
   whose power is in the skies.

³⁵You are awesome, O God, in your
   sanctuary;
   the God of Israel gives power and
   strength to his people.

Praise be to God!

The text for this fine national anthem was the call of Numbers 10.35, and it is possibly a hymn to be set beside Psalm 24 amid the rejoicing of those high days which saw the beautiful symbol of the Ark restored to Jerusalem.

David regarded those days as the joyous summit of his career. The frontiers were at peace ('His enemies are scattered', is the correct translation of verse 1). The lands of Israel's enemies were, and still are, in fact, arid lands (6). The great procession, with the Ark glittering at the head, was like another Exodus (7, 8), followed by echoes of the conquest, even of Deborah's song (4, 5, 8, 13, 16).

In verses 13 and 14 is a poetic allusion which escapes us. The imagery is of the land's hills and heights—Sinai, Hermon, Bashan, Zion and, even if the language is correctly rendered, some pictures in the poet's mind, especially the gold and silver dove, is obscure. The violent language of verses 19 to 23 must be read in the context of war-ridden borderlands, and it should be noted that another sort of conquest gathers up the poem, the scattering of those who love war, and the old vision of world peace (28-31).

69 DESOLATION

Save me, O God,
  for the waters have come up to my neck.
²I sink in the miry depths,
  where there is no foothold.
I have come into the deep waters;
  the floods engulf me.
³I am worn out calling for help;
  my throat is parched.
My eyes fail,
  looking for my God.
⁴Those who hate me without reason
  outnumber the hairs of my head;
many are my enemies without cause,
  those who seek to destroy me.
I am forced to restore
  what I did not steal.

⁵You know my folly, O God;
  my guilt is not hidden from you.
⁶May those who hope in you
  not be disgraced because of me,
  O LORD, the LORD Almighty;
may those who seek you
  not be put to shame because of me,
  O God of Israel.
⁷For I endure scorn for your sake,
  and shame covers my face.
⁸I am a stranger to my brothers,
  an alien to my own mother's sons;
⁹for zeal for your house consumes me,
  and the insults of those who insult you
    fall on me.
¹⁰When I weep and fast,
  I must endure scorn;
¹¹when I put on sackcloth,
  people make sport of me.
¹²Those who sit at the gate mock me,
  and I am the song of the drunkards.
¹³But I pray to you, O LORD,
  in the time of your favour;
in your great love, O God,
  answer me with your sure salvation.
¹⁴Rescue me from the mire,
  do not let me sink;
deliver me from those who hate me,
  from the deep waters.
¹⁵Do not let the floodwaters engulf me
  or the depths swallow me up
  or the pit close its mouth over me.

¹⁶Answer me, O LORD, out of the goodness
  of your love;
  in your great mercy turn to me.
¹⁷Do not hide your face from your servant;
  answer me quickly, for I am in trouble.
¹⁸Come near and rescue me;
  redeem me because of my foes.

¹⁹You know how I am scorned, disgraced
    and shamed;
  all my enemies are before you.
²⁰Scorn has broken my heart
    and has left me helpless;
 I looked for sympathy, but there was none,
    for comforters, but I found none.
²¹They put gall in my food
    and gave me vinegar for my thirst.

²²May the table set before them become a
    snare;
  may it become retribution and a trap.
²³May their eyes be darkened so that they
    cannot see,
  and their backs be bent for ever.
²⁴Pour out your wrath on them;

let your fierce anger overtake them.
²⁵May their place be deserted;
   let there be no one to dwell in their
      tents.
²⁶For they persecute those you wound
   and talk about the pain of those you hurt.
²⁷Charge them with crime upon crime;
   do not let them share in your salvation.
²⁸May they be blotted out of the book of life
   and not be listed with the righteous.

²⁹I am in pain and distress;
   may your salvation, O God, protect me.

³⁰I will praise God's name in song
   and glorify him with thanksgiving.
³¹This will please the LORD more than an
      ox,
   more than a bull with its horns and
      hoofs.
³²The poor will see and be glad —
   you who seek God, may your hearts live!
³³The LORD hears the needy
   and does not despise his captive
      people.

³⁴Let heaven and earth praise him,
   the seas and all that move in them,
³⁵for God will save Zion
   and rebuild the cities of Judah.
 Then people will settle there and possess
      it;
³⁶ the children of his servants will inherit it,
   and those who love his name will dwell
      there.

This sombre psalm, in such stark contrast with the glad confidence of its predecessor, is quoted in the New Testament six times. It is not a Messianic psalm, for much of it could not possibly refer to Christ. Here and there the disciples discerned some apt reference, and remembered verse 9, for example, when the Lord cleansed the temple. But for the ancient heading, which commands respect, the piece could be attributed to Jeremiah. There are six passages in that harassed prophet which echo the language. Was it a Davidic psalm passed in agony through Jeremiah's experience?

Encompassing evil is a flood, almost overwhelming (1). Unbearable distress has followed sin and folly (5). But though all has been set right in penitence before God, man's contempt and violence continue to rage against him. Was this after David's notorious adultery (6-12)? To claim God's acceptance in such a desperate situation took some courage (13-20). It is sometimes difficult to forgive ourselves for the sins God has forgiven us—but such is our privilege, and in that undoubted blessing lies peace of mind and healing.

70 IN NEED

Hasten, O God, to save me;
 O LORD, come quickly to help me.
² May those who seek my life
 be put to shame and confusion;
may all who desire my ruin be turned
 back in disgrace.
³ May those who say to me, 'Aha! Aha!'
 turn back because of their shame.
⁴ But may all who seek you
 rejoice and be glad in you;
may those who love your salvation always
 say,·
 'Let God be exalted!'

⁵ Yet I am poor and needy;
 come quickly to me, O God.
You are my help and my deliverer;
 O LORD, do not delay.

Apart from some small changes the five verses of this little hymn are from Psalm 40, which also occupies a place near the end of a book of the Psalter. Perhaps the editor had some liturgical purpose in mind. Perhaps he thought of the verses as a fitting summary for the closing themes of Book 2. But can language which touches the heart be too often repeated?

71 OLD AGE

In you, O LORD, I have taken refuge;
  let me never be put to shame.
²Rescue me and deliver me in your
    righteousness;
  turn your ear to me and save me.
³Be my rock of refuge,
 to which I can always go;
 give the command to save me,
  for you are my rock and my fortress.
⁴Deliver me, O my God, from the hand of
    the wicked,
  from the grasp of evil and cruel men.

⁵For you have been my hope, O Sovereign
    LORD,
  my confidence since my youth.
⁶From birth I have relied on you;
  you brought me forth from my mother's
    womb.
  I will ever praise you.
⁷I have become like a portent to many,
  but you are my strong refuge.
⁸My mouth is filled with your praise,
  declaring your splendour all day long.

⁹Do not cast me away when I am old;
  do not forsake me when my strength is
    gone.
¹⁰For my enemies speak against me;
  those who wait to kill me conspire
    together.
¹¹They say, 'God has forsaken him;
  pursue him and seize him,
  for no one will rescue him.'
¹²Be not far from me, O God;
  come quickly, O my God, to help me.
¹³May my accusers perish in shame;
  may those who want to harm me
  be covered with scorn and disgrace.

¹⁴But as for me, I shall always have hope;
  I will praise you more and more.
¹⁵My mouth will tell of your righteousness,
  of your salvation all day long,
  though I know not its measure.
¹⁶I will come and proclaim your mighty
    acts, O Sovereign LORD;
 I will proclaim your righteousness, yours
    alone.
¹⁷Since my youth, O God, you have taught
    me,
and to this day I declare your marvellous
    deeds.
¹⁸Even when I am old and grey,
  do not forsake me, O God,
till I declare your power to the next
    generation,
your might to all who are to come.

¹⁹Your righteousness reaches to the skies,
    O God,
  you who have done great things.
  Who, O God, is like you?
²⁰Though you have made me see troubles,
    many and bitter,
  you will restore my life again;
 from the depths of the earth
  you will again bring me up.
²¹You will increase my honour
  and comfort me once again.

²²I will praise you with the harp
  for your faithfulness, O my God;
 I will sing praise to you with the lyre,
    O Holy One of Israel.
²³My lips will shout for joy
  when I sing praise to you —
  I, whom you have redeemed.
²⁴My tongue will tell of your righteous acts
    all day long,
 for those who wanted to harm me
  have been put to shame and confusion.

*The writer appears to be old (9), and
through a long life has kept the faith (18).
He has his trials (2, 10, 11, 13). He knew the
psalms well, especially 22, 31, 35, 40. It
could be Jeremiah, so frequently under
attack, weaving remembered words into a
'new song'. There are no fewer than ten
quotations, and it is a good habit to do as
this writer has done, and store the mind
with memorised scriptures.*

54

The writer knew that 'it is not the beginning of a matter, but the ending thereof that bringeth the true glory.' It should be our prayer, too, to end our days well and to know that the evening has temptations as stern and strong as those of the morning. Enemies have multiplied as the years thinned friends, and he passionately desires not to flag in his running. 'Always' is his theme (3, 14).

'Old age has yet its honour and its toil.' John wrote his Gospel in his nineties. Memorise verse 18 against that day and pray for 'some late lark singing'.

72 THE KING'S SON

Endow the king with your justice,
O God,
the royal son with your righteousness.

[2] He will judge your people in
righteousness,
your afflicted ones with justice.
[3] The mountains will bring prosperity to the
people,
the hills the fruit of righteousness.
[4] He will defend the afflicted among the
people
and save the children of the needy;
he will crush the oppressor.

[5] He will endure as long as the sun,
as long as the moon, through all
generations.
[6] He will be like the rain falling on a mown
field,
like showers watering the earth.
[7] In his days the righteous will flourish;
prosperity will abound till the moon is
no more.

[8] He will rule from sea to sea
and from the River to the ends of the
earth.
[9] The desert tribes will bow before him
and his enemies will lick the dust.
[10] The kings of Tarshish and of distant
shores
will bring tribute to him;
the kings of Sheba and Seba
will present him gifts.
[11] All kings will bow down to him
and all nations will serve him.

[12] For he will deliver the needy who cry out,
the afflicted who have no one to help.
[13] He will take pity on the weak and the
needy
and save the needy from death.
[14] He will rescue them from oppression and
violence,
for precious is their blood in his sight.

[15] Long may he live!
May gold from Sheba be given to him.
May people ever pray for him
and bless him all day long.

[16] Let corn abound throughout the land;
on the tops of the hills may it sway.
Let its fruit flourish like Lebanon;
let it thrive like the grass of the field.
[17] May his name endure for ever;
may it continue as long as the sun.

All nations will be blessed through him,
and they will call him blessed.

[18] Praise be to the LORD God, the God of
Israel,
who alone does marvellous deeds.
[19] Praise be to his glorious name for ever;
may the whole earth be filled with his
glory.
Amen and Amen.

[20] This concludes the prayers of David son
of Jesse.

*A psalm 'for Solomon' (KJV) or a psalm 'of
Solomon' (RSV)—both titles have been
suggested. It could be an anthem written
by David (20) and set aside for his son's
coronation. It is a fine poem, whether one
or two kings had a part in it.*

*Righteousness and justice for the poor
(1-4), are a passion in the Old Testament,
and how true the instinct. The land where
the needy are denied justice is a land
sliding to decay. Shakespeare knew verse
6. The good king's beneficence 'droppeth
as the gentle rain from heaven'.*

*The next verses inspired the hymn:
'Jesus shall reign . . .' From 'sea to sea' (8)
meant in those days from the Atlantic to the
Indian Ocean. Solomon's 'ships of Tarshish'
knew those trade-routes. It is the old
dream again of a peace without frontiers.
Such wonder, if man would, God could
give (18).*

73 I WAS ENVIOUS

Surely God is good to Israel,
to those who are pure in heart.

²But as for me, my feet had almost slipped;
I had nearly lost my foothold.
³For I envied the arrogant
when I saw the prosperity of the wicked.
⁴They have no struggles;
their bodies are healthy and strong.

⁵They are free from the burdens common to
man;
they are not plagued by human ills.
⁶Therefore pride is their necklace;
they clothe themselves with violence.
⁷From their callous hearts comes iniquity;
the evil conceits of their minds know no
limits.

⁸They scoff, and speak with malice;
   in their arrogance they threaten
      oppression.
⁹Their mouths lay claim to heaven,
   and their tongues take possession of the
      earth.
¹⁰Therefore their people turn to them
   and drink up waters in abundance.
¹¹They say, 'How can God know?
   Does the Most High have knowledge?'

¹²This is what the wicked are like —
   always carefree, they increase in wealth.

¹³Surely in vain have I kept my heart pure;
   in vain have I washed my hands in
      innocence.
¹⁴All day long I have been plagued;
   I have been punished every morning.

¹⁵If I had said, 'I will speak thus,'
   I would have betrayed this generation of
      your children.
¹⁶When I tried to understand all this,
   it was oppressive to me
¹⁷till I entered the sanctuary of God;
   then I understood their final destiny.

¹⁸Surely you place them on slippery
      ground;
   you cast them down to ruin.
¹⁹How suddenly are they destroyed,
   completely swept away by terrors!
²⁰As a dream when one awakes,
   so when you arise, O Lord,
   you will despise them as fantasies.

²¹When my heart was grieved
   and my spirit embittered,
²²I was senseless and ignorant;
   I was a brute beast before you.

²³Yet I am always with you;
   you hold me by my right hand.
²⁴You guide me with your counsel,
   and afterwards you will take me into
      glory.
²⁵Whom have I in heaven but you?
   And being with you, I desire nothing on
      earth.
²⁶My flesh and my heart may fail,
   but God is the strength of my heart
   and my portion for ever.

²⁷Those who are far from you will perish;
   you destroy all who are unfaithful to you.
²⁸But as for me, it is good to be near God.
   I have made the Sovereign LORD my
      refuge;
   I will tell of all your deeds.

This beautiful composition picks up the theme of Psalm 37, a theme as old as Habakkuk and Job. Why do the good suffer, and the evil so often prosper? Malachi asked the same question and, like Habakkuk, found an answer in faith and a glimpse of immortality (Malachi 3.14-18).

The storm of resentment is over when the psalm opens (1), but it had been a sharply fought encounter with doubt (2, 3). Doubt is a common experience, and a man can hardly be said to know true faith who has never known doubt. It is what is done with doubt that matters. It cannot become a way of life, or the spirit crumbles.

Asaph took his eyes from the horrible spectacle of prosperous wickedness which seemed to mock his faith (4-16), and sought the place of prayer. Like Habakkuk he had his 'watch-tower'. From this vantage point he saw life in true perspective. He saw his own folly. He saw strutting evil for the poor and transient thing it is. He has learned a lesson—the mind is safe only when 'stayed on God'.

74 GOD'S ENEMIES

Why have you rejected us for ever,
O God?
Why does your anger smoulder against
the sheep of your pasture?
²Remember the people you purchased of
old,
the tribe you redeemed as your
inheritance –
Mount Zion, where you dwelt.

³Pick your way through these everlasting
ruins,
all this destruction the enemy has
brought on the sanctuary.
⁴Your foes roared in the place where you
met with us;
they set up their standards as signs.
⁵They behaved like men wielding axes
to cut through a thicket of trees.
⁶They smashed all the carved panelling
with their axes and hatchets.
⁷They burned your sanctuary to the ground;
they defiled the dwelling place of your
Name.
⁸They said in their hearts, 'We will crush
them completely!'
They burned every place where God
was worshipped in the land.

⁹We are given no miraculous
signs; no prophets are left,
and none of us knows how long this will
be.
¹⁰How long will the enemy mock you, O
God?
Will the foe revile your name for ever?
¹¹Why do you hold back your hand, your
right hand?
Take it from the folds of your garment
and destroy them!

¹²But you, O God, are my king from of old;
you bring salvation upon the earth.
¹³It was you who split open the sea by your power;
you broke the heads of the monster in the waters.
¹⁴It was you who crushed the heads of Leviathan
and gave him as food to the creatures of the desert.
¹⁵It was you who opened up springs and streams;
you dried up the ever-flowing rivers.
¹⁶The day is yours, and yours also the night;
you established the sun and moon.
¹⁷It was you who set all the boundaries of the earth;
you made both summer and winter.

¹⁸Remember how the enemy has mocked you, O LORD,
how foolish people have reviled your name.
¹⁹Do not hand over the life of your dove to wild beasts;
do not forget the lives of your afflicted people for ever.
²⁰Have regard for your covenant,
because haunts of violence fill the dark places of the land.
²¹Do not let the oppressed retreat in disgrace;
may the poor and needy praise your name.

²²Rise up, O God, and defend your cause;
remember how fools mock you all day long.
²³Do not ignore the clamour of your adversaries,
the uproar of your enemies, which rises continually.

This 'Asaph' psalm is not necessarily from the choirmaster of David's day. It was a composition of a certain style, and it is used here for a lament as sad as Jeremiah ever wrote. It might fit more than one occasion but best of all the desolation of Jerusalem by Nebuchadnezzar. 'Laments' are a common form of literature, found in Greek and Gaelic poetry and elsewhere.

But what put agony into this poet's spirit was the spectacle of lovely and consecrated things smashed by brutish vandals (6-8), and the apparent carelessness or helplessness of God before such blasphemy and desecration (1—4). God has nothing to say (9), did nothing (10, 11), for all the faith which had held him mighty (12-17).

The psalm, unusually, ends without relief. It takes us deeply into the agony of the Exile, and we who read with more illumination must thank God for stronger light on that other dimension—eternal life.

75 GOD THE JUDGE

We give thanks to you, O God,
we give thanks, for your Name is near;
men tell of your wonderful deeds.

²You say, 'I choose the appointed time;
it is I who judge uprightly.
³When the earth and all its people quake,
it is I who hold its pillars firm.   *Selah*
⁴To the arrovant I say, "Boast no more,"
and to the wicked, "Do not lift up your
horns.
⁵Do not lift your horns against heaven;
do not speak with outstretched neck." '

⁶No one from the east or the west
or from the desert can exalt a man.
⁷But it is God who judges:
He brings one down, he exalts another.
⁸In the hand of the LORD is a cup
full of foaming wine mixed with spices;
he pours it out, and all the wicked of the
earth
drink it down to its very dregs.

⁹As for me, I will declare this for ever;
I will sing praise to the God of Jacob.
¹⁰I will cut off the horns of all the wicked,
but the horns of the righteous shall be
lifted up.

This psalm might come from the jubilant months following the retreat of Sennacherib, a grand occasion of confidence and vindication. Perhaps even the assassination of the Assyrian king eighteen years later inspired it.

Uplifted horn and stiffened neck are symbols of pride (5, 6). 'Do not flaunt your power, nor speak with wanton presumption', is R.K. Harrison's rendering, and arrogant nations still 'put their trust in reeking tube and iron shard'. But God is judge of all such 'valiant dust that builds on dust' (6-8). The psalm ends with a shout of gladness (9, 10).

The same moral law still rules. God has never repealed it, and our own age has seen nations drink the cup of verse 8. It is not yet drained.